The Beekeepers' Story

written by Shelia Black

illustrated by Mark A. Mohr

McGraw-Hill
School Division

New York   Farmington

It is late March and spring has already come to southern New Mexico. The brown desert landscape is dotted with bits of green. Bright flowers are blooming among the brush. For Gordon and Laura Solberg, who own a small piece of land beside the Rio Grande, the work year is just beginning.

The Solbergs are beekeepers. They keep about ninety hives scattered in a sheltered cove up and down this part of the Rio Grande Valley. You don't usually imagine bees in a desert like this, but in fact honeybees live in an incredible variety of landscapes around the world, from tropical rainforests to northern plains. The colonies of bees in Gordon and Laura Solberg's hives are exactly like the bees that live in the wild.

Each of the Solbergs' hives contains up to sixty thousand bees. Each hive also contains a single queen who is the mother of the hive and lays all the eggs. You can easily spot the queen of a hive because she is longer and larger than the others. Most of the bees are female worker bees, and a much smaller number are male bees or *drones*, who exist only to mate with the queen.

Some workers, called *house bees*, tend the hive and take care of the queen and her eggs. Others are *field bees* or *foragers* who fly out of the hive to collect pollen or nectar. A field bee may fly as far as five miles from the hive and make as many as ten trips a day. On each trip she collects pollen from at least a hundred flowers; she stores the pollen in honey sacks in her legs and carries it back to the hive.

3

There, the pollen is transferred to the house bees who in turn pass the pollen from bee to bee until it is transformed into honey by enzymes in the bees' bodies. The honey is then stored in the six-sided cells of the honeycomb.

When a honeycomb cell is filled with honey, the bees top it with beeswax secreted from their bodies. This honey will provide the workers and the newly hatched larvae with food. Instead of honey, a few cells in a honeycomb will contain a food called *royal jelly*. Royal jelly is made in the glands of workers' bodies. A diet of royal jelly enables the queen bee to lay her eggs.

Bees interest scientists because they are so well organized and are extremely social. For instance, when a bee stings you it is usually to defend its hive; while the bee-sting may hurt you, it actually kills the bee. Biologists call this behavior *altruism*, which means goodwill. A bee cannot survive without its hive.

Now that spring is here, the bees are stirring. It looks as if it will be a good year for them, and for the Solbergs, because it has been an unusually wet winter. "The rain means we're seeing a lot of spring wildflowers," Laura says. "This means we should get a good crop of spring wildflower honey."

The Solbergs' bees produce about five different kinds of honey, depending on the time of year and what kind of pollen they are collecting. Today Gordon and Laura are cleaning out their honey house in preparation for the expected spring wildflower honey harvest.

The honey house is where they extract honey from their hives; it is a long, low building crowded with all kinds of supplies. "That's how you can tell a serious beekeeper," Gordon jokes. "They always have a mess of beekeeping stuff lying around."

Hive frames are piled against the wall. Each hive is housed in a *hive body*, which is a wooden box as weathered as driftwood that holds up to ten frames. These frames look like picture frames, but instead of paintings they contain sheets of wax or plastic foundation on which bees build the wax cells of the hive. The frames slide into the hive like drawers in a dresser.

Next to the frames "supers" are stacked. Supers are built like hive bodies, only smaller; they are placed on top of hives and provide space for the bees to store their extra honey, which is the honey the beekeepers will harvest. Laura says that during the course of the year she and Gordon will often put as many as nine supers on top of a hive. This is to provide the bees with enough space to store all the honey they are making.

While Gordon wipes off the machinery, Laura cleans newspaper up off the floor; there is not much to pick up today. Laura says that when they are in the middle of a big honey harvest there will often be as many as fifty to a hundred sheets of newspaper on the floor. That's because it's impossible to harvest honey without some spilling, and every time it spills they quickly spread newspaper over it. "If we didn't, we'd end up a sticky mess," says Laura, "or even more of a sticky mess than we do anyway!"

There are two pieces of equipment the Solbergs use to extract their honey; the first is called an *uncapper*. Many beekeepers just use a knife to cut the wax caps off the honeycomb cells of a frame, but the Solbergs have a machine to do it. It consists of rows of chains, which whirl around, lifting the wax caps off the cells of a frame almost instantly.

Once the honeycomb cells are uncapped, the frames are placed in the honey extractor. This machine is shaped like a large metal barrel, and inside it is a rack which holds the frames upright. The Solbergs' extractor holds twelve frames at a time. When Gordon or Laura turn it on, the extractor whirls the frames around much like the spin cycle in a washing machine. This spinning pulls the honey out of the honeycomb cells; it then runs down the sides of the tank and out the *spigot*, or tap, at the bottom.

The Solbergs collect the honey in clean five-gallon plastic buckets, and then the honey is filtered to remove any bits of beeswax or other impurities. Afterwards, Laura and Gordon bottle it in glass jars, plastic jugs, and "honey bears," label it, and place it in the storeroom next door. Laura says one of her favorite things about beekeeping is stepping into the storeroom when a harvest is over and seeing the shelves and shelves of golden honey jars all lined up in the cool darkness.

This first harvest of spring wildflower honey is usually the Solbergs' smallest; it is followed by the mesquite harvest. "The mesquite blooms in May," Laura explains. "Mesquite honey is by far the most popular with our customers so that is usually our busiest time of year."

Mesquite wood is well known among barbecue fans for giving barbecued meat a fine smoky flavor. Mesquite honey, however, is a mild, beautiful, buttery-looking honey with a delicate fragrance. Laura claims mesquite flowers barely look like flowers at all, but more like fat green furry caterpillars, but the honey they make is among the finest in the world.

When the Solbergs sell their honey at farmer's markets they always run out of mesquite honey first. Because there is so much mesquite in the desert, mesquite honey is also one of their largest harvests. In the middle of mesquite season, the Solbergs often extract 500 pounds of honey a day from their hives!

When the mesquite honey comes in, the Solbergs often work ten days straight to get it all harvested. The schedule is so tight because they need to bring the mesquite honey in before the salt cedar trees bloom in early June.

The flowers of the salt cedar tree are much prettier than mesquite blossoms, pink and feathery, but the honey from them is dark and strongly flavored. If the Solbergs' bees start consuming salt cedar before all the mesquite honey has been removed from the hives, their honey changes flavor, and it then must be sold as a blend. Many people don't like the taste of salt cedar honey but Laura says it is her favorite; she loves its dark, woodsy flavor.

After the salt cedar harvest, the alfalfa and cotton in the farmers' fields bloom in July and August, when the desert air is so hot it can sizzle. Many of these farmers pay the Solbergs to keep beehives on their farms to help pollinate their crops. The last honey harvest of the year is in September when, if there has been enough rain, the Solberg bees make honey from the summer wildflowers. Then comes winter, a quiet time for the Solbergs and for their bees.

The desert landscape turns brown and lifeless, and the bees ball up in their hives. Some beekeepers feed their bees sugar syrup to get them through the winter. Gordon thinks that's a disgrace, explaining, "Refined sugar isn't healthy for bees." Instead, he leaves his bees enough honey to keep the hives going until spring. After twenty-five years of beekeeping, he can tell if the bees have enough honey just by lifting a hive and feeling how heavy it is.

Gordon and Laura say this yearly schedule is one of the most interesting things about beekeeping. "We have to follow the bees," Gordon explains, noting that bees are wild animals, not domesticated or tame, like cows. "The way I see it, bees have been on this planet a lot longer than we have and are pretty set in their ways. A beekeeper's job isn't to control his bees, but to be ready for what they do."

For example, in spring when the hives are growing quickly, a beekeeper must watch for signs that a hive is about to swarm. When a hive gets too crowded, the colony splits, and half the hive flies off, along with the old queen. The bees that are left rebuild the hive around a new queen. However, it will take a year or two before this new young hive produces much honey.

A beekeeper can try to prevent swarming by adding more supers to give the bees more room, or by dividing the hive in two. They can also destroy the new queen cells, which the worker bees make when they are getting ready to swarm. Yet often no matter what a beekeeper does, the bees will swarm anyway.

Gordon says this is what makes beekeeping a challenge. You have to be alert and willing to learn from experience and Gordon says he is still learning. He usually keeps a small notebook in his pocket and in it he writes notes to himself about beekeeping: new things he's trying and observations about his bees.

Now, in the early spring, Gordon and Laura must check on their hives almost every week. They examine them for new brood, or young bees. If a hive seems short of brood, they may decide the queen is too old or too sickly and will have to "requeen" the hive. When they do this, they must order a new queen by mail from a supplier. The queen is shipped in a small wooden box along with the worker bees that care for her.

"When she arrives, we always get a call from the post office," says Laura, "The clerk will say in a worried-sounding voice, 'Mrs. Solberg, your bees are here. Can you come get them?' When Gordon and I arrive at the post office, they'll point to a far off corner and say 'Your bees are over there!' "

In recent years, the Solbergs have had to requeen many more of their hives because of the spread of South American "killer bees." These bees are much more aggressive than the sweet or Italian bees most American beekeepers work with. "A number of our hives have been colonized by them," Gordon says. "I've never yet had to destroy a hive because of it, but I've had a couple I wish I had." Now he avoids this by requeening his hives regularly, so the queens won't have a chance to mate with wild killer bee drones.

Gordon and Laura also check their hives for disease. Bees are host to several bacteria and parasites. The bacteria *American foulbrood* was once a problem for beekeepers, but now it can be avoided by medicating hives with an antibiotic called *terramycin*. A bigger problem today is a parasite called the *bee mite*, a tiny insect which infests bee hives. The current medicine appears to work for the Solbergs, but bee mites are quick to develop resistance to medication.

Whenever they check their hives, the Solbergs dress up in heavy canvas bee suits and bee gloves topped with hats and veils. They also use smokers, small metal devices that are filled with a burning substance. Whenever Gordon opens a hive, he blows smoke into it and the bees, thinking the hive is on fire, flail around filling their bodies with honey. Once stuffed, they find it almost impossible to sting. The Solbergs still get stung about twenty times a year, though almost never out in the field.

"Its funny," Gordon says, "beekeeping is hard work. By September, I'm ready for a rest, but once winter is over I'm always eager to get started working with my bees again." He likes the fact that as a beekeeper he is independent. "In farming today, the small guy has mostly been driven out by big business," he says, "but beekeeping can't be run that way. Each bee hive still must be taken care of by hand."

Gordon claims his bees help keep him curious about the world. For instance, he must pay close attention to the weather. "In the desert, a lot of rain sometimes falls on a small piece of ground," he notes. "As a beekeeper you have to be aware of that because it means a few of your hives might have a lot of wildflower honey."

Laura agrees, "You learn that if enough rain doesn't fall, the seeds just won't bloom, and that means we won't get our honey harvest. Being a beekeeper makes me feel as if I have a foot in two worlds. I see how fragile and complicated nature is, and I see that by ignoring nature or trying to control it, people may be upsetting balances they don't even know exist."

Today, though, the world does seem in balance. The honey house is clean and ready for the next harvest. Bees from the hives in the Solbergs' yard are flitting out to gather pollen, spreading wildflowers as they go. In the hives, cells are slowly filling with honey, light and dark, strong and mild, honey that reflects the land where it was made.